NAVIGATING SINGLE PARENTHOOD

A pocket guide depicting my journey through healing and growth: with space for your own notes

WRITTEN AND ILLUSTRATED BY

MARIA HELENA AHLBECK

CONTENTS

INTRODUCTION

Abuse comes in many forms, affecting anyone, and children are often involved within families. My deepest experience of abuse occurred within my marriage. The truth is that the abuser is a deeply wounded individual who cannot see or does not want to confront their need for healing, as it is often too overwhelming for them to face. As the 'victim,' you are doing the only thing you can: managing damage control for everyone involved. You cannot and are not responsible for anyone else's healing, except for your own and, if applicable, your children's.

If you have reached the point of leaving, it means you have decided you can no longer accept the negative behaviours in your life—well done. It is well known that many people try to leave an abuser several times before they succeed, and I understand why. You need to know, unequivocally, that this is the right decision for you, that it is the only way forward, and that you have set up the right conditions to start your new life safely. Core behaviours of control from the abuser often include financial manipulation, and it is now time for you to regain control of this aspect of your life. Please understand that recovering from years of abuse will take time and effort, but it is possible to recover and thrive—my children and I are proof of that.

I am a survivor of an abusive marriage with my ex-husband. We were together for 15 years, married for 13, and have been divorced for nearly 10 years. I became increasingly unhappy over time and realised I needed to leave him five years before I actually did. This reflects the slow and painful realisation of his undiagnosed Narcissistic Personality Disorder (NPD). I knew about NPD as it was becoming more widely discussed, and I observed and researched it extensively. It was a heavy and frightening discovery.

My inability to change things immediately was partly due to my low self-esteem and disbelief that this was happening. The passing of my mother was the final significant trigger that prompted me to move forward. Throughout our marriage and after our divorce, I learned a great deal about life, my place in it, and my identity as a woman, mother, sister, daughter, and wife. I chose to heal myself from that point onwards. Now, I can speak with him face-to-face because I have changed for the better and have established clear boundaries.

This does not mean it is easy; I still get triggered by him. However, I manage myself much better now, and the reality is that we are parents to two children and want the best for them.

In my opinion, there are no set rules for how long a relationship should last, whether married or unmarried. Every situation is unique. I believe that when the lessons have been learned and the relationship no longer serves either partner, it is time to move on.

I have come to understand the importance of letting go with grace, especially for the sake of the children. The end of a marriage is not a failure; it simply means the relationship has run it's course. This booklet is intended for single parents, including men, women, and others. I will use the term 'partner' to encompass all of these for simplicity.

This guide has been created because I felt it might be helpful to share my experience with others emerging from an abusive relationship, whether emotional or physical, and with children.

In the following five chapters, I will discuss what I have learned about living as a single parent as effectively as possible for our two children, now 20 and 16—one in their third year at university and the other in her final year at high school.

They were only 10 and 6 years old when we left, and since then, they have thrived academically and emotionally in everything they have chosen to pursue. For now, I want to congratulate you on making the decision to seek a better life for yourself, your former partner, and your children, as I know how incredibly challenging this decision can be.

Your notes:

....

....

....

....

....

....

....

Will you ever forgive yourself and stop feeling stupid and ashamed about what has happened to you?

It took me a long time to recover from what happened because the toxicity was deeply ingrained in both of us. For me, it was about time and finding people along my path who had been through, if not the same, remarkably similar situations. We had much to discuss.

This was where I initially found deeper healing—realising that I was not alone and that many others had been deceived on such a profound level. Toxic people are skilled at manipulating relationships in a slow, deep, and subtle way, so it makes sense that uncovering all of this takes time. However, I am here to tell you that you will get there and feel a million times better about yourself in time. You will also learn to forgive them, as this is part of the lesson that needs to be learned. If you do not forgive them, you will only perpetuate the pattern in the future.

Your notes:

ONE

A list of things I did before, during, and after my children and I left my abusive relationship.

1. I sought help from family and friends to transport our belongings. I couldn't pack before leaving and had to do this under immense duress, alone, once I had made it clear we were leaving.

2. I contacted Women's Aid, the crucial support organisation in the UK for female victims, which also offers support for male and other victims. They are extremely experienced and have fantastic resources, including for children if any are involved. I received immediate weekly counselling and was also offered Barnardo's by the police as another contact for domestic abuse situations, although I never used them.

3. I found a criminal lawyer through word of mouth who provided me with advice. It was very helpful to have someone outside my family assess my situation clearly and legally during the initial upheaval and trauma.

4. I returned to teaching and, my family helped by taking my children to school, enabling me to continue working. This was fundamental for me to rebuild and regain my self-esteem.

5. I maintained a routine for my children to ensure as much normality as possible.

Managing parenting with your former partner

The way we communicated was often very upsetting for everyone, and from the beginning of our separation, it became more volatile. When I left with the children, I told him we would return the following day for our belongings. However, he would not open the door, and when he did, it was unpleasant. I was obliged to call the police to intervene, and only then would he let me in to retrieve our belongings. It was a very sad day, but he was clearly very ill, and I had no other way of making him understand that he couldn't prevent us from accessing our belongings, no matter how angry and distraught he was.

I knew how important it was to keep the lines of communication open between us. However, we argued very easily at first because the toxicity between us was so deep. I eventually learned to rely on texts and emails as the 'safe mode' because calls would easily devolve into abuse between us both, becoming dangerous for everyone involved.I also learned to stick to factual information, feeling stronger when receiving and responding to him because my emotions in texts and emails only distracted from the relevant task at hand, which was to organise the children or finances.

Over time, we became calmer and managed to ensure that activities continued as planned. It is not a fail-safe method; challenging situations still arise, as they do in life. Nowadays, if necessary, I will call or speak face to face, although I avoid this if I can, for my own well-being.

The challenge of the children's emotions

The children's emotions were, of course, very delicate at this time. They were trying to navigate their own feelings of loss and how to interact with each parent, which was unfamiliar territory for them too. I found it challenging and frightening, and I made mistakes constantly. However, I knew I had to keep going and keep them talking to me. They were very tired of the fight-or-flight response themselves and looked to me for answers, which was exhausting.

I also did not fully realise the depth of the pain our children were experiencing because I was in it myself, so I lacked objectivity. Regardless, finding our new home was crucial, and it marked the beginning of the healing process for everyone involved.

Living Between Different Homes

Living between homes was a massive change, particularly for the children, as they moved between spaces to be with each partner for a period each week. This required meticulous planning, organisation, and monitoring.

During the official separation, the solicitors had to assess my ability to parent, given that domestic abuse was the cause.

I became the 'primary caregiver' to the children because their father was unable to fulfil this role. My sister was rigorously questioned by the solicitor to determine this designation for me. The girls only spent a few months staying with their father in his new home, which meant that the time I had begun to value for myself was consumed by their constant presence. I had to rethink how to carve out time for myself. I arranged for childminders, and fortunately, family members helped out for a few years, saving me money and ensuring the children were surrounded by familiar and safe faces.

The Challenge of Managing the Children's Activities

I often felt many negative emotions towards my ex-husband. However, I had to start coming to terms with these feelings, as they affected me, our children, my organisation, and our daily lives. Counselling helped me begin managing these emotions and limited the number of people with whom I discussed my personal situation.

I shared a schedule of activities and pick-up times with my ex-husband. The girls and I discussed the week or month ahead daily and, the night before, I reminded them of what was coming so they could process and pack what they needed for the following day. The girls quickly adapted and took initiative!

They packed for themselves, and I always suggested they bring a soft toy for comfort when they stayed with their father. School meetings were challenging as we were together in front of the children's teacher, which made me feel very vulnerable since he was a very convincing actor. I was afraid of being judged and unheard, and over time, I learned to remain silent unless necessary. I also arranged private meetings with their teachers, deputy head, and headteacher as needed to inform them of our situation from the children's and my perspective. The children were included in these discussions so they knew where and who the safe spaces and people in school were.

I also arranged for the children's care unit from Women's Aid to take them to a children's group at the after-school club once a week. This group provided a space where children could come together to learn about abuse and support one another. One of our girls went on a trip away from home, as she was old enough to spend a week without contact with either of us, except for text messages in case of emergencies. This was one of the toughest and most painful weeks for me, as she had never been away from either of us before. However, I realised she needed this experience.

Your notes:

How do you heal yourself and hold onto your sanity during the early months and years?

Having only had counselling in the initial stages of my breakup and separation, I can attest to how much I relied on the support offered by both Women's Aid and my GP referral system.

Both were invaluable, and I started to look forward to these sessions each week. I felt myself unburdening in front of them, even if I wasn't sure what the 'right' thing to say was; the words would come anyway. As the months passed, my body eased after each session, and although just attending the sessions helped, I initially struggled with feelings of failure, which took a long time to diminish.

Years later, when I added Medical Intuition to my therapy mix, I felt I was finally getting to the root of my issues. This was a significant breakthrough during many sessions, and I began to feel like a brand-new woman. Everyone has their own preferred therapy, and these two approaches worked best for me.

Your notes:

TWO

How I Moved Home, Managed Shopping, and Paid Bills

The children and I moved into a small house, which I was fortunate to afford due to my mother's passing. I made it clear that this space was only for the children and me, as late as possible in the process. His behaviour towards me and the children during and after my mother's passing was very unpleasant, so by that point, I was focused on surviving and protecting us.

From then on, my job's salary would cover the bills, so I moved everything to the lowest cost possible. I explained to my children from the start how things had to be at that time, and they accepted it. I never promised them anything I couldn't deliver, a lesson my mother taught us, which meant my children understood their situation. They initially had two activities, but over time, this had to be reduced to one, and they made the most of it.

Creating a monthly budget helped me, and I set up standing orders and direct debits for what I could, ensuring I only used the services I needed and cancelled those I didn't. I had to be ruthless. I accessed government funding and advice where possible. In Scotland, there is Child Benefit and a Scottish Child Payment fund offering monthly payments for each child under 16, which transitions to Education Maintenance Allowance (EMA) thereafter.

I also sought funding from my Union to support myself and my children after I fell ill and had to leave work. I set up my accounts clearly so that I knew what was going where and when. I maintained a current account and two savings accounts, managing day-to-day finances effectively. Gaining control over my finances was vital after having it taken from me for 15 years.

After discussing with trusted family and friends, I prepared for both a divorce and a 'Minute of Agreement' to stipulate the amount of money I would receive monthly to support the children and the division of their care. My ex-husband refused to cooperate as it involved spending money to compile it. I insisted on it because it was a legal document, but I did not realise he would simply ignore it.

Costing about £2,000 to produce, it became worthless to me as I could not afford legal intervention to enforce it. Neither did he want to go to court to avoid paying legal fees, so I approached at least two financial advisors and an experienced solicitor to help me understand my situation.

Food shopping is essential and needs to be healthy, so I was selective. Organic and free-range food can be expensive. If you can afford it, great; however, for us, the expense did not justify the means. The only free-range items I bought were eggs and chicken, as I questioned the quality of these foods otherwise.

The rest of our food was budget-friendly, and my children and I remain healthy by prioritising fresh or frozen fruit and vegetables as essentials.

How Do You Cope Managing Finances After Being Restricted for So Long?

You may be surprised at how quickly you adapt, simply because you haven't had the chance to do so before. Regaining control over your finances can be empowering. Personally, I felt like Superwoman when I managed to use my salary to cover expenses that I previously had to ask for. I noticed that my ex-husband struggled with my newfound confidence and tried to belittle me, feeling threatened by it. That was when I realised how much he had underestimated me and was shocked by my actual resilience.

You will still make mistakes, but you will learn to navigate them better and better, which will help you feel more empowered. Watch yourself grow.

Your notes:

THREE

How to Deal with Challenging Behaviour from Your Children

I had just removed my children from a place they considered home, with one parent left behind. My guiding principle was to simply love them, as that was what they needed the most.

Over time, I observed them adjusting and allowed them the space and time to process everything. Life was never going to be easy for us, but all I could do was take it one day at a time for both them and myself.

When arguments broke out, I would often blame myself and feel deeply guilty. However, children need to vent, and now I was the one they would target because they felt safe doing so. Before this, they had been too scared to speak up, so I had to recognise that this behaviour was a positive sign, step back, and steel myself, no matter how painful it was.

There were wonderful moments when either of the girls would quietly approach me, wrap their arms around me after a bout of misbehaviour, and apologise with tears. We would both end up crying, and I would hold them as long as possible to feel better because we both needed it. I let them hold on for as long as they needed to.

We would eventually chat and often laugh about something silly, and I knew we were moving in the right direction when we could smile, laugh, and be silly together.

There were times when deeply challenging things happened, some harder than others. My approach remained the same: I loved my children and offered myself as the constant emotional safety net that they couldn't get from their father. This could be very painful and often felt like failure on my part. However, I realised that I had only failed them if I was not available to provide my presence and make them feel safe in their own home. Having already achieved that, I learned to breathe easy and trust that, in time, things would improve.

What Do You Do If Your Child Screams and Doesn't Stop?

Managing persistent screaming can be extremely exhausting for a single parent. Depending on the reason for the challenging behaviour, there are a few strategies to consider. Firstly, try not to feel embarrassed (easier said than done, I know!), as all children go through this. In my opinion, it is a way for them to test boundaries, vent, or express exhaustion.

As a mother, I found it effective to let the child continue until they tire themselves out, as they eventually will. They will likely need a cuddle afterwards, and I always made sure they knew I was there for that. If you are on a tight deadline, try to let it go if possible, as children need their parent more than deadlines. If letting go isn't an option, focus on yourself and your breathing. Staying calm helps to eventually calm your child, as they sense and mirror your emotions. The quicker you can calm your own breathing, the sooner you can enlist their co-operation.

An interesting tactic I learned from someone else, though I never had the opportunity to use it, involves dealing with tantrums in the supermarket. If your child throws a tantrum in an aisle and won't stop, you, as the parent, get down on the ground with them and start screaming too! The reaction of horror from your child as you mimic their behaviour can make them realise how it appears to others, and they will often stop. It requires courage on your part but can be very effective.

Your notes:

Your notes:

FOUR

How I Loved Myself While Parenting with My Ex-Husband

Having just broken free from an abusive partner, I felt broken and deeply vulnerable. I felt compelled to give endlessly to my children and often felt unimportant in the grand scheme of things. I experienced a lot of guilt and still had very little time to myself. At the time, I didn't recognise this as a result of co-dependent behaviour.

As mentioned earlier, I accessed counselling through Women's Aid and complemented this with counselling via my GP, which proved very helpful in the long term. Initially, when the children went to their father's, finding time for myself felt daunting because I was so accustomed to being with them constantly. I eventually realised that I needed to use this time wisely as a chance to reconnect with myself and my friends. When he could no longer have them at his home, I felt pressured and manipulated once again.

I knew I couldn't afford to lose my personal time, so I arranged childcare with family when possible, friends, or others who could help from time to time, finances permitting. I also made sure to have evenings to myself or with friends. During that time, I attended dance classes, which was important as it took me out of the house. Over time, I also incorporated running and walking into my routine, up to 5k, which really helped to maintain my strength.

As a trained dancer, I needed activities that encouraged endorphin flow, which is why running was beneficial. It was also free, making it a practical choice. Additionally, I enjoyed massages and acupuncture, which provided wonderful physical and mental support from trusted practitioners.

Regarding friendships, some people understood my situation, while others did not. The right friends will stay with you. I was surprised by some individuals whom I believed respected me but who took my ex-husband's side in conversations. This revealed their lack of understanding of abuse and disrespect for my perspective. I realised they were in my circle for the wrong reasons, so I had to learn to remove them gently but firmly.

Blinded by preconceived notions, I initially thought they had my back until I realised they didn't. Once I made the decision to let them go, I felt better and recognised that I had made the right choice. Letting them go graciously contributed to my increased health and happiness.

How to Move Forward as a Single Person?

At this stage, I had already felt single for several years, so it was not a new reality, but rather a fact I had to face once I finally moved out. It was very scary, lonely at times, and overwhelming. However, whenever I asked myself if I would prefer to return to what I left behind, the answer was always a resounding no. This provided me with the guidance to keep moving forward. I sought opportunities to be with other families so the children could play and enjoy activities, and I would have a friend to chat with as well.

In terms of looking for a new relationship, I know many people seek one quickly. In my experience, I attempted to connect with others within the first two years after the separation and ended up very hurt. I realised that taking the time to heal myself first was the best approach.

Your notes:

How Do You Know What Loving Yourself Looks Like?

When I was first asked this question, I was perplexed and didn't understand what it meant; it almost seemed irrelevant. This was a reflection of how out of touch I was with myself after years of being 'the wife and mother' and largely ignored by my ex-husband.

It took years for me to realise that I had completely lost myself and that rediscovering who I was would require focus. I had observed other women going out with friends or alone and was initially shocked that they could do this, as it seemed unthinkable to me—until it wasn't.

Once separated and divorced, I learned how to go out by myself—whether to the cinema, a restaurant, or on a solo break. The freedom from answering questions, dealing with arguments, or preparing meals for the children was a joy. I discovered how to enjoy being alone, watching a movie, preparing my preferred meal, or inviting a friend or two over for an evening together.

Your notes:

FIVE

I Followed My Heart and Dreams

My parents always taught me that life is a gift and that we each have individual talents we can use to live our lives to the fullest. In my experience, it's often only when we feel unhappy that we are compelled to reassess our lives and figure out what isn't working for us.

I became disillusioned with my marriage as the passion and desire to make it work faded, especially as the abuse escalated. For me, it took the passing of my mother, a divorce, and later, serious illness (the first two events together and the third several years later) to awaken to my reality and dreams. I felt a strong need to show my children that one should not remain in a situation where one is unhappy.

Once I recovered (I first had to test the waters by returning to work to determine the source of my unhappiness, which was my job), I found the courage to make a drastic change by resigning due to ill health. This decision opened up the possibility of creating a new life. Letting go of my past allowed a new future to emerge, leading me to train as a healer. I found this prospect incredibly exciting. As I progressed through my training, I discovered that I didn't have to relinquish all that I had learned and done up until that point—my healing style, my art, dance, and teaching. Instead, I could incorporate all these elements into my new work. Once this realisation hit, I was the happiest I had ever been.

I then dedicated myself to building my new business as a healer, creating content, and following what felt right for me, while seeking out appropriate resources to move forward.

I won't say it's always been easy to establish a new business and life for myself. Similarly, my children have sometimes struggled with the choices I've made. However, the need to change my lifestyle was too profound to ignore, and ignoring oneself and one's body can lead to unhappiness and long-term illness, as I learned the hard way in 2018.

As my children have grown older, they have come to understand and respect that their mother is also a human being with her own dreams and desires. They now see me standing up for what I believe in, both as a person and a healer. They help me when they can and recognise how much healthier I am now compared to before. While they may not agree with everything I do, it's important for us all to accept each other as we truly are, rather than living a lie that would only lead to unhappiness.

Helping others has always been my goal, and now, drawing on all the experience and knowledge I've gained as a mother, artist, dancer, and teacher, I feel guided in what I am meant to do moving forward. I am certain that staying in a job that made me ill was not an option because I couldn't fully be myself. I believe we are all here to be happy and healthy, and achieving this is not only attainable but absolutely possible!

What Are Your Dreams?

What is in your heart, and have you ever followed it before without feeling guilty?

In my experience, learning to love yourself enough to step away from society's expectations of what a single parent should be doing for their children takes time. Discover what you want for yourself and work towards that.

The truth is, children observe what we do rather than what we say. My advice is to ask yourself what you want for the rest of your life, regardless of your role as a parent, and how you can make that happen. Illness forced me to reassess my goals and focus, so why not avoid illness and reevaluate what you want for the rest of YOUR life?

Your life needs purpose and dreams, and in my opinion, that is what truly matters. Your children will pick up on your excitement and follow your lead.

Sending you love and light as you continue your journey....

Your notes:

RECOMMENDED BOOKS

- "Codependent No More" by Melody Beattie

- "The Amazing Liver and Gall Bladder Flush"
  by Andreas Moritz

- "Metaphysical Anatomy" Volume 1 by Evette Rose

AUTHOR BIOGRAPHY.

Maria H. Ahlbeck is an artist, dancer, and certified Medical Intuitive. Growing up in an artistic family, Maria developed a passion for drawing, painting, and contemporary dance. Her high school's vibrant art department inspired her to pursue a career in art, leading her to study Illustration and Printmaking.

While teaching in Vietnam, she immersed herself in the local culture and studied dance with the Vietnam National Opera and Ballet Company. This experience laid the foundation for her formal training, which she pursued for three years at the Scottish School of Contemporary Dance in Dundee and then at De Montfort University in Leicester.

After moving to Norway and then England, Maria balanced her roles as a teacher, mother, and caregiver. Following personal and professional challenges, she retrained as a Medical Intuitive, blending her artistic background with holistic healing. Now based in Scotland, Maria integrates her passions for art, dance, and holistic medicine into her daily life while maintaining a fulfilling balance between her career and family.